UNITED STATES
SUPREME COURT
LIBRARY

Stephen Breyer

by Paul J. Deegan

ABDO & Daughters
Minneapolis, MN

Published by Abdo & Daughters, 4940 Viking Drive, Suite 622, Edina, Minnesota 55435.

Copyright © 1996 by Abdo Consulting Group, Inc., Pentagon Tower, P.O. Box 36036, Minneapolis, Minnesota 55435 USA. International copyrights reserved in all countries. No part of this book may be reproduced in any form without written permission from the publisher.

Printed in the United States.

Cover Photo credit: Bettmann Photos
Interior Photo credits: Wide World Photos
Edited by Bob Italia

Library of Congress Cataloging-in-Publication Data

Deegan, Paul J., 1937-
    Stephen Breyer / by Paul J. Deegan.
        p.   cm. -- (United States Supreme Court library)
    Includes index.
    Summary: Provides details in the life and career of jurist Stephen Breyer and his nomination to the
        Supreme Court.
    ISBN 1-56239-464-9
        1. Breyer, Stephen G., 1938—Juvenile literature. 2. Judges--United States—Biography—Juvenile
        literature. 3. United States.
        Supreme Court—Biography—Juvenile literature. [1. Breyer, Stephen G., 1938- . 2. Judges. 3.
        United States. Supreme Court--Biography.] I. Title. II. Series United States Supreme Court library
        (Series).
KF8745.B69D44   1996
347.73'2634--dc20
[B]
[347.3073534]
[B]
                                                                                    96-3859
                                                                                    CIP
                                                                                    AC

Table of Contents

Choosing a Successor

On April 6, 1994, 85-year-old Supreme Court Justice Harry Blackmun announced his retirement after 24 years of service. When the announcement came, President Bill Clinton's administration was ready with a list of possible replacements.

White House Counsel Lloyd Cutler led the search for Blackmun's successor. He had performed similar tasks for President Jimmy Carter. Each candidate's character, temperament, and legal ability would be considered.

Maine Democratic Senator George Mitchell was President Clinton's first choice to replace Blackmun. Mitchell had already announced his decision to retire from the Senate at the end of 1994. The 60-year-old Mitchell had helped President Clinton's unsuccessful campaign to pass health care reforms. But on April 12, Mitchell announced that he was not interested in the appointment.

Senate Majority Leader George Mitchell of Maine.

Interior Secretary Bruce Babbitt and U.S. Appeals Court Judge Richard Arnold of Little Rock, Arkansas, were next on the list. Babbitt now was seen as the favorite to fill the court vacancy. But the former governor of Arizona said he was content serving in the President's Cabinet.

Judge Arnold was a longtime friend and law professor of President Clinton.   The 58-year-old Arnold was a graduate of Yale University and Harvard Law School. He had been active in public-interest work before becoming a judge. But President Clinton knew he would be criticized for naming a resident of Little Rock to the court, so he decided against it.

Judge Jose Cabranes, Chief of the U.S. District Court in Connecticut, was also considered. The 53-year-old Cabranes, a native of Puerto Rico, would be the first Hispanic Supreme Court justice. Also mentioned were Judge Amaslya Kearse of the U.S. Court of Appeals in New York and U.S. Solicitor General Drew Days, both of whom were black. Another strong candidate was Stephen Breyer, Chief Judge on the First United States Court of Appeals in Boston.

The Candidate

The suspense ended 37 days after Blackmun resigned. On May 13, 1994, Clinton chose Judge Breyer to the Supreme Court. The President revealed his choice at a White House ceremony so quickly scheduled that Breyer could not attend. He had been notified of his selection only an hour before the ceremony.

When he spoke to reporters in Boston that same day, Breyer said he would try "to make the average person's ordinary life better. That's an incredible challenge." He also stated he felt "very humble simply thinking about it."

The 55-year-old Breyer was a respected jurist, uncontroversial, a moderate, and a legal scholar. "Without dispute," President Clinton said, "he is one of the outstanding jurists of our age." The President praised Breyer for his legal and political knowledge.

Senator Edward Kennedy, Breyer's longtime friend and chief sponsor, and Senator Orrin Hatch, a Republican from Utah, endorsed Breyer. Republican Senator Bob Dole also had publicly endorsed Breyer.

A year earlier, Breyer had been considered for the court vacancy to which President Clinton had named Ruth

Bader Ginsburg. Breyer was in the hospital recovering from an auto accident when President Clinton called him for an interview.

Breyer was the favored nominee. But he was passed over because of a minor tax violation. Breyer had failed to pay Social Security taxes for a part-time housekeeper. Though the amount involved was small, the revelation was awkward for the Clinton Administration. The President's first two nominees for attorney general had withdrawn from consideration because of similar problems.

Opposite page: Senator Edward Kennedy escorts Stephen Breyer, President Clinton's Supreme Court nominee.

Brilliant Legal Scholar

In the spring of 1994, Breyer was again considered a strong candidate. Not only was he a safe choice, he had the skills, including a clear grasp of the law. He also had much respect for the constitutional and legal rights of the American people.

Breyer was called a brilliant legal mind by some of his peers. Lawyers who had worked with Breyer in New England also praised him as bright and scholarly. Regarding the unpaid Social Security taxes for the household worker, Breyer had paid the back taxes. The payment was refunded because the Internal Revenue Service (IRS) ruled he never owed the taxes in the first place.

Consumer activist Ralph Nader criticized the nomination. "He is no friend to workers, consumers or the environment," Nader said. "He's never met a corporate merger he didn't like." Liberal Democrat Senator Howard Metzenbaum from Ohio said Breyer had favored big business and a weakening of government regulation of business.

Few Risks

Breyer's appointment offered the President many rewards and few risks. He expected the Senate to confirm Breyer as the nation's 108th Supreme Court justice. The Senate's role in appointing Supreme Court justices is explained in the U.S. Constitution. It states that the President nominates and, "by and with the advice and consent of the Senate," appoints judges of the Supreme Court.

Senate Judiciary Committee action is the first step in the nomination process. The Committee, whose members included Senators Kennedy and Metzenbaum, would recommend Breyer's nomination to the entire Senate.

Breyer was no stranger to Washington, D.C., nor to the Supreme Court. Out of law school, he had been a clerk to Associate Justice Arthur Goldberg.

The Senate confirmed Breyer to the federal court in 1980. President Carter had nominated him before losing the next presidential election. The Senate Judiciary Committee conservatives liked Breyer so much that they supported his confirmation. He was the only Carter nominee to be approved by the Senate.

Now in 1994, Breyer was expected to be approved. Senator Dole said, "Nobody's going to lay a glove on him."

Political Fighting

No one is nominated to the Supreme Court solely because of his or her ability. Politics also play an important role.

It is difficult to predict how a new Supreme Court justice will rule on any particular case. Sitting on lower courts, judges follow precedent—a court decision, often by the Supreme Court, that is used as a standard in a later, similar case. Once someone is named a Supreme Court justice, he or she takes part in setting precedent that the lower courts will follow. Justice Blackmun was a good example of how unpredictable a justice could be.

Big Shoes to Fill

"Big shoes to fill," Breyer said in May 1994 about replacing Justice Blackmun. Republican President Richard Nixon had appointed Blackmun to the Supreme Court in 1970. It was Nixon's third try at filling that court vacancy. The Senate had rejected his two prior nominees.

Chief Justice Warren Burger recommended Blackmun to Nixon. Blackmun and Burger had been friends since grade school. Blackmun's voting record as a federal appellate judge was similar to Burger's, who was considered a conservative thinker.

But once on the high court, Blackmun emerged as one of the court's leading liberals. He wrote the Supreme Court's landmark opinion in the 1973 *Roe v. Wade* decision, establishing a woman's right to have an abortion.

President Clinton looks on as retiring Supreme Court Justice Harry Blackmun addresses reporters.

Returning to Washington

Two days after President Clinton announced his selection, Judge Breyer came to Washington with his wife and their daughter Chloe, the oldest of the Breyer's three children.

Breyer arrived at the nation's Capitol. He jumped into an airport taxi, but Clinton aides stopped the taxi and got Breyer into a White House van. They did not want a taxi in the White House arrival ceremony for the Supreme Court nominee. The Breyer's dined with President Clinton and Hillary Rodham Clinton, then spent the night at the White House.

The following day, President Clinton presented Breyer to the public in a White House Rose Garden ceremony. The President said Breyer had extraordinary intellectual talents, and would bring to the court "the heart and head of a reformer." The President also praised Breyer's "abiding sense of decency and unswerving dedication to ensuring liberty and justice for all."

Breyer said he would defend the law's letter and spirit. "The Constitution and the law must be more than mere words," he stated. "I will certainly try to make law work for people."

Stephen Breyer introduces his family to the Senate Judiciary Committee; from left are daughters Chloe and Nell, son Michael and wife Joanna.

Two months later, Breyer sat before the
Senate Judiciary Committee. He presented himself as a
moderate judge with liberal leanings. He expressed his
great interest in making government work.

He spoke often about the Constitution. It "… is a
document that basically wants to guarantee people rights
that will enable them to lead lives of dignity." Breyer said
the Constitution "foresees over the course of history that a
person's right to speak freely and to practice his religion
is something that is value, is not going to change."

Breyer promised to keep in mind how court rulings
affect individual lives. He always looked for the economic
consequences of government actions. Economics, he
said, must take second place to saving lives.

Judge Breyer made known his respect for
Congress—more than any recent court nominee. In

information given to the Senate Committee, Breyer wrote about the Supreme Court's role regarding reform and problem-solving. These roles, he stated, were best left to the other two branches of government, Congress and the presidency. The courts were not well equipped to make such decisions. But he expressed the belief that the courts must become involved when the legislative and executive branches perform poorly.

During his opening statement, Breyer addressed the issue of whether he may have had a financial conflict of interest in several cases he decided. These were toxic waste cases he dealt with as a federal appeals court judge in Boston. The supposed conflict arose from Breyer's membership in a British insurance syndicate. Lloyd's of London underwrote insurance for corporations facing the costs of cleaning up pollution.

Breyer told the Senate Committee that his participation in those cases did not present any conflict of interest. But, he said, to eliminate any conflict, he would remove himself from all financial interest in insurance companies.

After Breyer completed 3 days of testimony, the Judiciary Committee's 18 members—10 Democrats and 8 Republicans—voted 18-0 to recommend his court appointment to the entire Senate.

On July 29, 1994, the Senate approved Breyer's nomination as an associate justice of the Supreme Court with an 87-9 vote.

Breyer was sworn in as a Supreme Court justice on August 3, 1994. The private ceremony took place at the Vermont summer home of Chief Justice William Rehnquist. Rehnquist conducted the swearing-in. Justice Breyer repeated the oath of office at a public White House ceremony on August 13, 1994.

California Native

Stephen Breyer was born August 15, 1938, in San Francisco, California, to Anne and Irving Breyer. His father spent 40 years, much of them as an administrator, in the San Francisco public school system. His mother's father was a cobbler in Poland. He came to the United States in 1900. Education was very important to his mother. To her, it had meant so much more than material comforts.

When he was a teenager, Breyer had jobs digging ditches and waiting tables. He had gone to public elementary schools in San Francisco and attended Lowell High School.

Breyer's college choice was Stanford University in nearby Palo Alto, California. After graduating from Stanford with honors, Breyer attended Oxford University in England. He received another bachelor's degree with honors from Oxford's Magdalen College.   During his time at Oxford, Breyer became fond of British ways and Joanna Hare. Her father, Lord Blakenham, once led Britain's Conservative Party.

Breyer returned to the United States to attend Harvard Law School in Cambridge, Massachusetts. Breyer received his law degree, again with honors, in 1964. When Breyer took his seat on the 9-member Supreme Court 30 years later, he became one of 4 justices who were graduates of Harvard Law School. The others were Justices Anthony Kennedy, Antonin Scalia, and David Souter.

In 1964-1965, Breyer served his clerkship for Justice Goldberg. As Goldberg's clerk, Breyer helped write the majority opinion for the famous Supreme Court decision *Griswold v. Connecticut,* which recognized for the first time a constitutional right to privacy.

Breyer moved on to congressional staff work where, as a Senate aide, he designed the legislation Congress passed in 1978 to deregulate the airline industry.

Breyer returned to Harvard Law School in 1967 as an assistant professor. That same year, he married Joanna Hare. He would remain in Boston for 27 years.

Breyer became a full professor in 1970 and taught at Harvard until 1980. During the last four years, he also was a professor at Harvard's Kennedy School of Government. He remains a lecturer at Harvard.

While teaching at Harvard, Breyer continued a presence in the nation's Capitol. He won praise for his role in 1973 as an assistant prosecutor on the Watergate Special Prosecution Force. He served as a special counsel to a Senate Judiciary Committee's subcommittee in 1974-1975. He was chief counsel to the Judiciary Committee in 1979-1980.

Breyer left Harvard but remained in Boston when he became Judge Breyer on December 10, 1980. After ten years as a judge on the U.S. Court of Appeals for the First Circuit, he was named Chief Judge. He held this post in 1994 when President Clinton nominated him for the nation's highest court.

Breyer's wife is a psychologist who worked at the Dana-Farber Cancer Institute in Boston. Besides Chloe, the Breyers have two other children: Nell, born in 1971, and Michael, born in 1974.

Though a wealthy man, Breyer often bicycled to work in Boston. His shirt collars were sometimes frayed and he wore sweaters with holes in them. Despite his intelligence, he also has a reputation for being absentminded. The newest Supreme Court justice is also a jogger. His other recreational interests include cooking and reading.

Potential Consensus-Builder

Justice Breyer joined a court that was divided on important issues. Chief Justice William Rehnquist and Justices Scalia and Clarence Thomas were on the conservative right. Blackmun and Justice John Paul Stevens were on the liberal left. The other four justices—Sandra Day O'Connor, Kennedy, Souter, and Ginsburg—were considered unpredictable.

On the day he presented Judge Breyer to the public in Washington, President Clinton said that his nominee was a proven consensus-builder—someone who helps the Court reach an agreement. No one had played such a role on the court since 1990. The last consensus-builder was Justice William Brennan, who retired in 1990.

Opposite page: President Clinton jogs with Stephen Breyer.

Justice Breyer believed consensus on the court was important. He said it results in more understandable opinions.

Justice Breyer's views put him near the center of the court. His testimony before the Committee suggested that he would line up with Justice Ginsburg and bring middle-of-the-road views to a conservative court.

Supreme Court nominee Stephen Breyer facing the Senate Judiciary Committee.

The Work Begins

The newest justice took his seat when the court began its 1994-1995 session on October 3, 1994. On the day his appointment was confirmed by the Senate, Justice Breyer had said, "The responsibility ... is awesome, rather humbling." But, he said, "I'll do my best."

Historically, the new Supreme Court justices seldom have had much impact beyond their votes. However, during his first term, Justice Breyer took an active part in oral arguments before the court.

Sitting at the far right of the bench—the place given to the least senior justice—Breyer often waited until a lawyer's allotted time was almost over. Then he started his questioning. He asked questions in paragraphs. He summed up where the arguments had been and where he wanted them to go. When it came time to write an opinion, Breyer did it on a computer.

When the Supreme Court's 1994-1995 term ended on June 29, 1995, Justice Breyer had lined up with Justices Stevens, Souter, and Ginsburg on four cases. On all four

Supreme Court Justice Antonin Scalia, right, administers the Supreme Court oath to Stephen Breyer, August 13, 1994.

decisions, these four justices were on the losing side of a 5-4 decision. The term was called one of the most conservative in 40 years. The court limited federal affirmative action programs. Public funding of a religious activity was allowed for the first time. The court reined in federal judges presiding over school desegregation. And on its final day of the term, the court made it much more difficult to bolster black voters' political clout.

As he began his second term as a Supreme Court justice on October 2, 1995, the opinion expressed by a newspaper editorial writer in 1994 was only beginning to be evaluated. Stephen Breyer, the newspaper had said, was "a thinking judge, with a shot of greatness."

Glossary

activist: Someone who supports or is against a certain cause and takes action.

administration: A large group of people who assist and advise the president.

aide: Assistant.

bachelor's degree: A degree given by a four-year college upon graduation.

Cabinet: A small group of people who help the president run the country.

campaign: A number of connected activities aimed at a common goal.

candidate: A person who seeks some office or honor.

Capitol: The building in Washington, D.C., where the U.S. Congress meets.

clerk: A person who keeps and files records.

clout: Influence or power.

cobbler: A person who makes or repairs shoes.

conflict of interest: A conflict between private interests and the official responsibilities of a person in a position of trust.

Congress: The lawmaking body of the U.S. government, which consists of the Senate and the House of Representatives.

consensus: General agreement.

conservative: A person who believes in less government, less taxes, and little change.

Constitution: A document that states the principles and laws of the United States.

credentials: Evidence of one's talents.

Democrat: A member of the Democratic Party; one who practices social equality.

deregulate: To remove government control.

economics: The science that deals with producing, distributing, and using goods.

endorse: To give verbal or written approval.

evaluated: Carefully examined and judged.

intellect: Ability to learn and reason.

Interior Secretary: A Cabinet member in charge of the country's internal affairs.

Internal Revenue Service (IRS): A branch of the federal government responsible for collecting taxes.

judge: A public official appointed or elected to hear and decide cases in a court of law.

jurist: A judge.

landmark: An important event.

legislative: Lawmaking.

liberal: A person favorable to progress, big government, and social reforms.

moderate: Someone who does not have extreme views.

nominate: Proposed by someone for a job or public office.

nominee: One who has been nominated.

peer: A person of the same, rank, or ability.

politics: The work of government.

precedent: A court decision that is used in a later, similar case.

professor: A teacher of the highest rank in a college or university.

prosecutor: A lawyer who brings legal action against a defendant.

psychologist: A person who is an expert in psychology, the science of the mind.

Republican: A member of the Republican Party; one who favors less government involvement in people's lives.

reform: To make better; improve.

regulation: Controlled by the government.

scholar: A person having much knowledge.

Senate: A lawmaking assembly.

Senator: A member of the United States Senate.

Social Security: Money withheld from workers' pay that is used for retirement benefits, disability, unemployment, and social welfare.

Supreme Court: The highest court of the federal government.

Supreme Court Justice: A judge on the Supreme Court.

syndicate: A group of people or businesses that work together for a common goal.

tax: Money paid by people for the support of the government and the cost of public works and services.

temperament: A person's nature.

toxic: Harmful.

underwrite: To guarantee financial support.

U. S. Court of Appeals: A higher federal court that retries lower court cases.

Watergate: A political scandal involving the Nixon administration at the Watergate Hotel in Washington, D.C.

White House Counsel: The president's lawyer.

Index

K

Kearse, Amaslya 6
Kennedy, Ted 8, 12
Kennedy, Anthony 22, 25
Kennedy School of Government 23

L

law degree 22
law school 6, 12, 22, 23
lecturer 23
liberals 10, 18, 25
Little Rock (AR) 5, 6
Lloyd's of London 19
Lowell High School 21
lower courts 13

M

Magdalen College 22
Massachusetts 22
Metzenbaum, Howard 11, 12
Mitchell, George 4, 5
mother 21

N

Nader, Ralph 10
New England 10
New York City 6
Nixon, Richard 14
nomination 10, 12, 20, 23
nominees 9, 12, 16, 18, 25

O

oath of office 20
O'Connor, Sandra Day 25
Oxford University 21, 22

P

Palo Alto (CA) 21
Poland 21
presidents 4, 6-9, 11, 12, 14, 16, 23, 25
President's Cabinet 5
public elementary schools 21
Puerto Rico 6

R

recreational interests 24
Rehnquist, William 20, 25
religious activity 28
Republicans 20
reputation 24
Roe v. Wade 14

S

San Francisco 21
Scalia, Antonin 22, 25
Senate 4, 8, 11, 12, 14, 20, 22, 27
Senate Judiciary Committee 12, 18, 19, 23
Social Security 9, 10
Souter, David 22, 25, 28
Stanford University 21
Stevens, John Paul 25, 28
Supreme Court 4, 6, 7, 11-14, 16, 19, 20,
    22, 24, 27, 28

T

tax violation 9
teenager 21
Thomas, Clarence 25

U

U.S. Court of Appeals 6, 23
U.S. District Court 6
Utah 8

V

Vermont 20

W

Washington, D.C. 16, 25
Watergate Special Prosecution Force 23
White House 4, 7, 16, 20

Y

Yale University 6